Blockchain Revolution

How Cryptocurrency is Shaping the Future of Finance

Table of Contents

Chapter 1. Introduction

In this Special Report, we delve into the complex, yet captivating world of blockchain, bringing an enlightening investigation of the "Blockchain Revolution: How Cryptocurrency is Shaping the Future of Finance". We journey through the intricate workings of this game-changing technology, gently unpacking its mechanisms in an understandable, straightforward manner without any technical jargon and esoteric terms. We explore the impact of cryptocurrencies on the finance sector, investigating its potential to revolutionize not just how we transact, but how we live. This is a transformation no less fundamental than the advent of the internet itself. Join us, as we demystify the convolutions of blockchain technology, highlighting its potential benefits and the challenges ahead, thereby preparing you to confidently navigate this new frontier in finance. This report will serve as your handy guide to understand, participate and thrive in this imminent revolution of digital currency. Welcome aboard for an enlightening journey.

Chapter 2. Understanding the Basics: Blockchain, Cryptocurrency, and Decentralization

Before plunging headfirst into this new financial frontier, it is essential to establish a firm foundation of understanding. This includes the fundamental components of this revolution: blockchain, cryptocurrency, and decentralization. These key elements each play a role, like gears in a complex machine, all contributing to what may be the significant overhaul of financial transactions and digital security in history.

2.1. The Mechanism: Blockchain

Blockchain serves as the backbone of cryptocurrency. It is a continuously growing list or 'chain' of records, otherwise known as 'blocks', which are linked and secured using cryptography. Each block typically contains a cryptographic hash (a kind of digital "fingerprint" of the previous block, a timestamp, and transaction data.

This piece of data architecture was designed to be secure, unalterable, and transparent. Data stored in a block cannot retroactively be tampered with without the alteration of all subsequent blocks, which requires majority network collusion — thereby enabling secure data storage and transfer. Transparency is attained as every participant in the blockchain network has access to the entire blockchain.

Blockchains are usually distributed, meaning there is no central point where the data resides. This enhances security as there is no "single point of failure" susceptible to hacking. Data stored in a blockchain is instead distributed across all nodes (participants) in the network, making it virtually unfeasible to alter the data across all replicated versions of the chain.

2.2. The Currency: Cryptocurrency

Cryptocurrency, as its name suggests, is a type of currency. But unlike the paper notes and metal coins that are the traditional forms of money, cryptocurrency is purely digital or 'virtual'. It uses cryptography for security, making it extremely tough to counterfeit.

Bitcoin, the first ever cryptocurrency, was invented in 2009 by an individual or group named 'Satoshi Nakamoto'. Instead of being issued by a central government or agency, Bitcoin is mined - a process where powerful computers perform complex calculations to validate transactions and add them to the blockchain.

Cryptocurrencies are built on blockchain technology, utilizing its security, transparency, and distributed nature. The inherent cryptographic security enables secure transactions, the transparency allows all transactions to be traced and verified, while decentralization eliminates the need for a central authority to govern the currency or transactions.

2.3. The Principle: Decentralization

Decentralization is a foundational pillar of blockchain technology and cryptocurrencies. Rather than store all information in one central hub, blockchain distributes the information across a network of interconnected nodes. Each node has a copy of the entire blockchain, and consensus must be achieved across these nodes for new blocks to be added to the chain.

This principle of decentralization makes blockchain remarkably resistant to corruption or tampering from a single source. Moreover, it promotes data democratization by ensuring that every participant in the network can access and verify information. As such, it enables peer-to-peer transactions to be made without the need for intermediaries like banks or governments.

While decentralization provides security benefits, it does pose challenges. Reaching consensus across the network can be time-consuming and resource-intensive, slowing the speed of transactions. Furthermore, the anonymity provided by decentralization presents legal difficulties, as it may facilitate illicit activities.

2.4. Reshaping Finance

While it might seem complicated at first, the mechanisms of blockchain, the nature of cryptocurrency, and the principles of decentralization are all critical to this growing world of digital finance. As they continue to evolve and mature, these elements are reshaping how we perceive and execute financial transactions.

Blockchain offers a means to maintain transparent, secure transaction ledgers; decentralization promises a world without the need for centralized authorities, while cryptocurrencies offer a new paradigm for executing and managing financial transactions.

However, this transformation isn't without its hurdles. Regulatory hang-ups, technological obstacles, and societal acceptance are just a few of the challenges standing in the way of widespread adoption.

This report seeks to understand these challenges, shedding light on the benefits and potential pitfalls of this rapidly evolving sector. With careful exploration of its intricacies, the journey through blockchain and cryptocurrency can lead to a future of incredible potential and unprecedented financial flexibility.

The potential for blockchain to revolutionize the financial landscape and beyond is vast. By making the technology accessible and demystifying the complexities, we equip ourselves to engage with and thrive in a future shaped by blockchain. This journey of understanding, exploration and engagement is vital as we stand on the precipice of this revolutionary transformation. The challenges, the promise, the potential – it awaits us all. Together, we will understand, participate and thrive in this imminent, transformative revolution of digital currency.

Chapter 3. Journey into Blockchain: A Detailed Walkthrough

Where laypeople see in blockchain technology an IT gimmick behind the Bitcoin buzz, technologists recognize a breakthrough with potential to change the world. So let's journey into the essence, workings, and implications of this radical technology.

3.1. Tech Explained – Blockchain Basics

Blockchain technology can be likened to a digital ledger where transactions are recorded chronologically and publicly. By design, a blockchain is resistant to modification of the data — it is an open, distributed ledger that can record transactions between two parties efficiently, transparently, and in a verifiable manner.

Each block contains a cryptographic hash of the previous block, a timestamp, and transaction data (generally represented as a Merkle tree). Once data has been recorded in a block, it becomes very difficult to change. This immutable and transparent nature is what makes blockchain so transformative.

3.2. Understanding the Complex yet Fascinating Blockchain Mechanism

At its core, a blockchain is a chain of blocks — but not in the traditional sense. Here, the word 'block' refers to digital information (or the 'block') stored in a public database (or the 'chain'). Blocks in a blockchain house data about transactions like the date, time, and the participants. Moreover, each block in a chain carries a unique code called a 'hash'. The hash differentiates it from every other block.

When a block stores new data, it is added to the blockchain. However, four things must happen:

- The transaction must occur.

- The transaction must be verified.

- The transaction must be stored in a block.

- The block must be given a hash.

Once all these processes are complete, the block can be added to the blockchain.

3.3. Rise of Cryptocurrencies – The First Use Case of Blockchain

The biggest and perhaps the most known application of blockchain technology is Bitcoin, the digital currency that rose to phenomenal fame in the financial world. Bitcoin, like other digital currencies, is decentralized and transactions involving it can be done anonymously - a fact that has powered its allure and also its critique. Unlike traditional currencies, there's no need for a central authority or government backing it making it truly global.

Every single Bitcoin transaction ever conducted forms part of the blockchain, which can be publicly accessed. This means that Bitcoin usage requires a degree of public disclosure, more so than is associated with traditional financial systems.

3.4. Blockchain Revolutionizing Financial Services

The potential of blockchain to disrupt the field of finance is substantial. By eliminating middlemen and creating trust, blockchain can democratize access to financial services, just as the internet revolutionized access to information. Few areas where blockchain can change the finance industry include:

- Peer-to-Peer Payments: Blockchain can enable speedier, cheaper, and more private P2P transactions.

- Remittances: The current average cost of remittances is high. Blockchain's direct transfers can significantly reduce these costs and increase speed.

- Clearing and settlement systems: These take time and money, a big part of which blockchain could usurp.

- Fundraising: Blockchain can democratize access to funding through ICOs or tokenization.

Blockchain is not only about Bitcoin or money. In essence, it is about securely transferring 'value' from one person to another, which could redefine how we do business.

3.5. Challenges and Road Ahead

While blockchain brings with it a sea of opportunities, it is not without its own set of challenges. Issues around governance, energy consumption, scalability, and legal and regulatory acceptance are worth mentioning.

Adapting to and adopting blockchain isn't something that will happen overnight. It will require a concerted effort by businesses, individuals, and governments. The transition is likely to be gradual and steady, not sudden and radical.

As we move ahead, blockchain won't just become a buzzword. Studies suggest that it has the potential to become a universal "source of truth". In a world where trust is being eroded, blockchain can act as a powerful antidote.

Thus, our journey into the captivating world of blockchain has illustrated just how it is set to shape the future of finance, ushering in a new era of digital transformation. As we navigate this new frontier, it is crucial to grasp the implications it holds, preparing ourselves to understand, participate and thrive in the blockchain revolution.

Chapter 4. Rise of Cryptocurrency: An Unprecedented Phenomenon

The birth of cryptocurrency, specifically Bitcoin, represents an unprecedented financial phenomenon that has successfully challenged traditional financial institutions and systems in their quest for dominance. In slightly over a decade, it has evolved beyond a nascent concept into a reality that is beginning to shape the future of finance.

4.1. Cryptocurrency: From Obscurity to Mainstream Revolution

Initially, the cryptocurrency world was a dark, mysterious domain reserved for tech-savvy individuals and groups. It was not widely understood, hence the public kept their safe distance. However, the situation has dramatically changed over the past few years.

The rise of cryptocurrency can be attributed to several key factors. The first is the allure of a decentralized system that operates outside the traditional banking framework. The decentralization of cryptocurrencies means transactions are carried out peer-to-peer without the need for an intermediary, enhancing the speed and cost-effectiveness of transactions.

The sophistication and agility of blockchain, the backbone technology behind cryptocurrency, is another key factor. Blockchain technology ensures security and transparency by recording all transactions in a chain of blocks, where the record can't be changed or deleted, thus reducing chances of fraud.

A third factor involves increased awareness and understanding. Over the years, significant effort has been placed in educating the masses about cryptocurrencies, their use, and their advantages. As more people learn about cryptocurrencies, they reciprocate with trust and adoption which fuels the growth of this sector.

4.2. The Phenomenal Rise of Bitcoin

To understand the rise of cryptocurrency, we must first look at Bitcoin, the innovation that pioneered the concept.

In 2008, an anonymous entity named Satoshi Nakamoto published a whitepaper on a cryptographic mailing list describing 'Bitcoin: A Peer-to-Peer Electronic Cash System'. This digital cash system aimed to create an Internet currency that would circumvent traditional banking systems, providing an avenue for seamless, inexpensive cross-border transactions.

Initial uptake was limited to internet enthusiasts who mined and transacted in bitcoins for novelty. Things started to change when Bitcoin was acknowledged as a legal means of payment in some significant platforms.

By 2013, Bitcoin saw a sharp rise in value, crossing the $1000 mark for the first time. This boom attracted the attention of the general public, as well as governments and financial institutions. Bitcoin's wild price volatility soon became a topic in mainstream media. Today, despite continuous market fluctuation, Bitcoin retains a solid following and is a marker for the overall state of the cryptocurrency market.

4.3. Emergence of Altcoins

Following Bitcoin's success, numerous other cryptocurrencies—often called altcoins, short for alternative coins—were created. Altcoins often aim to tackle the limitations of Bitcoin or wholly reimagine the possible applications of cryptocurrency.

A notable example includes Ethereum, founded by Vitalik Buterin in 2015, which introduced smart contract functionality. Smart contracts allow actors to automate transaction conditions on the blockchain, thus widening its usability beyond simple value storage and exchange. Ethereum's creation marked the dawn of an era of multiple cryptocurrencies, each with unique features and potential uses.

Their rise is characterized by market volatility, extreme highs and lows, seeming to mirror Bitcoin's path, albeit at a faster pace. These altcoins, like Bitcoin, captured worldwide attention. Investors' interest skyrocketed as altcoins offered a new frontier of possibilities for high-yielding investments.

4.4. Crypto-Assets and the Evolution of Digital Finance

The cryptocurrency revolution didn't stop at digital cash. Soon, additional crypto-assets emerged, such as tokens, introducing further advancements and complexity to the digital finance world. Tokens, unlike pure cryptocurrencies, can represent a wide spectrum of assets or utilities on the blockchain platform.

Furthermore, Decentralized Finance (DeFi) has exploded in popularity. DeFi relies heavily on the principles of blockchain and smart contracts, allowing traditional financial services like lending, borrowing, and earning interest to occur in a decentralized environment, bypassing the conventional metal-bound bank buildings and their intermediaries.

The advent of cryptocurrencies and their broader classification as crypto-assets could well be the tip of the iceberg. The future might see the tokenization of various assets, tangible and intangible, opening up a potential trillion-dollar market.

As we delve further into the rise of cryptocurrency, it's important to acknowledge the oft-overlooked volatility that accompanies this rapidly changing industry. Nonetheless, understanding its fluidity and unpredictability, as well as the potential disruptions it brings to traditional financial models, is vital to appreciate its transformative power.

4.5. Conclusion

The rise of cryptocurrency represents a decisive movement towards a future where trust in transactional exchange doesn't rely on centralized bodies but on decentralized communities and cryptographic verification. In its brief, turbulent history, cryptocurrency has shown a capacity to reshape the very fibers of commerce, creating a hitherto unthinkable system where financial control can reside with the people themselves.

Nevertheless, challenges in regulation, scalability, privacy, and acceptance still remain. As we journey further into this brave new world of digital finance, it's not just the promise but also the potential pitfalls of cryptocurrency we need to keep in clear view. This digital revolution brings with it an unmatched blend of opportunities and challenges that are set to redefine commerce and the very concept of money itself.

Chapter 5. Decoding Bitcoin and Ethereum: The Forerunners in Crypto Space

Decoding the fascinating world of digital currency begins at the source, with the genesis of it all - Bitcoin and Ethereum. These two cryptocurrencies were not only the frontrunners but have also paved the way for subsequent innovations in the blockchain landscape. Let's dive deep into their workings, impacts, and distinguishing features.

5.1. Bitcoin: The Genesis

Launched in January 2009 by an anonymous entity by the name of Satoshi Nakamoto, Bitcoin emerged as the first-ever implementation of blockchain technology, translating the abstract concept into a tangible phenomenon. Based on a white paper published by Nakamoto in 2008, Bitcoin exhibited a groundbreaking remedy to the double-spending problem that plagued the theoretical constructs of digital money.

NOTE Double-spending is a potential pitfall associated with digital cash where a user spends the same amount twice. Blockchain, with its impregnable record of transactions, provided a solution to this problem.

Bitcoin transactions are validated by a horde of online entities termed "miners". They utilize heavy computational power to solve complex mathematical problems - a process that seals the transaction records onto the blockchain.

Bitcoin became the first currency to confide trust in a decentralized system, i.e., it steered clear from the requirement for a central bank or government authority to oversee transactions. This revolutionary feature has led to Bitcoin being referred to as a decentralized peer-to-peer (P2P) electronic cash system.

5.2. Ethereum: More Than Just a Cryptocurrency

Unlike Bitcoin, Ethereum takes the game of blockchain beyond transactional purposes. Launched by Vitalik Buterin in 2015, Ethereum showcased blockchain's potential as a platform to build and enact "smart contracts".

NOTE Smart contracts are self-executing contracts where the terms of the agreement are directly written into lines of code. These contracts run on the Ethereum blockchain and execute automatically when specified conditions are met.

Ethereum brought forth a platform where developers could design and build their own decentralised applications (DApps) and create tokens for their own blockchain projects. Ethereum's native cryptocurrency, Ether, is used for transactions within the Ethereum network. It is the fuel that incentivizes miners to validate transactions and keep the engine of the Ethereum blockchain running.

5.3. Comparative Analysis: Bitcoin vs Ethereum

While the purpose of both Bitcoin and Ethereum is essentially the same, to decentralize transactions, their functions differ significantly.

Bitcoin's primary purpose is as a decentralized digital currency, enabling users to make transactions in a peer-to-peer network. The supply of Bitcoin is limited to 21 million units, which gives it a deflationary aspect and enhances its potential as a store of value.

On the other hand, Ethereum goes beyond the boundaries of transactions and provides a platform for developers to build DApps. The supply of Ether is not capped, which classifies it as an inflationary cryptocurrency.

5.4. The Influence and Impact

Over time, Bitcoin and Ethereum have undoubtedly influenced the trajectory of financial technology.

Bitcoin, with its promise of secure and anonymous transactions, has offered an alternative to traditional monetary systems, particularly in environments afflicted by hyperinflation or capital controls.

Ethereum has significantly impacted the world of contractual agreements and crowdfunding with its smart contracts and tokenization facilities. It has also influenced the growth of Decentralized Finance (DeFi), a fast-growing sector aiming to replace traditional finance with more transparent and accessible blockchain-powered solutions.

5.5. The Challenges Ahead

Despite their pioneering innovation, Bitcoin and Ethereum are not without challenges. From scalability issues to environmental concerns related to mining, there are hurdles yet to be resolved.

Bitcoin struggles with high energy consumption due to its mining processes; it's so high that Bitcoin mining's annual energy consumption has been compared to that of entire countries.

Ethereum, for its part, needs to overcome limitations in transaction throughput and speed. Although its shift to Ethereum 2.0 aims to solve scalability concerns using sharding and Proof of Stake (PoS) consensus algorithm, the full implementation is still in the works.

5.6. Conclusion

Although the crypto space is much more diverse today, Bitcoin and Ethereum remain indispensable. As the forerunners, they have not only offered unique solutions but also set the stage for future blockchain innovations. Despite the challenges, their potential and influence continue to shape the future of finance and beyond, standing testament to the power and flexibility of blockchain technology. This journey through the landscapes of these two pillars of cryptocurrency is an essential foundation to grasp the broader aspects of blockchain and the revolution it propels.

Chapter 6. Cryptocurrencies beyond Bitcoin: The New Digital Frontier

While Bitcoin is indeed the pioneer of cryptocurrencies, the blockchain technology it introduced has facilitated the emergence of a plethora of other digital currencies. Each one of these holds unique potential, promising to revolutionize different sectors besides the world of finance. By doing so, they are voraciously establishing their presence on this digital frontier.

6.1. The Genesis of Altcoins

Bitcoin was and remains the most famous cryptocurrency; however, developers and entrepreneurs have since created countless other digital currencies, often referred to as altcoins (alternative coins). These altcoins are either variants of Bitcoin, deriving from its open-sourced code, or are entirely fresh creations leveraging blockchain technology's fundamental principles. Litecoin, Ripple, and Ether are a few notable instances among thousands of such altcoins.

Litecoin, often described as silver to Bitcoin's gold, was released in October 2011 by former Google engineer Charlie Lee. Since Litecoin features a different hashing algorithm than Bitcoin, this altcoin validates transactions much more swiftly.

Ripple, or XRP, debuted in 2012. While it does provide a cryptocurrency for transactional purposes, Ripple's primary goal is to serve as a real-time settlement system for large financial institutions. Unlike Bitcoin and several other cryptocurrencies, Ripple doesn't require mining. The system's creators issued a set number of coins that decrease with each transaction, thus defeating counterfeiting attempts.

Ether, on the other hand, is part of a more ambitious endeavor. This altcoin serves as the token for the Ethereum platform, a decentralized software project aiming to facilitate the creation, deployment, and execution of smart contracts. These are digitized agreements that self-execute when predefined conditions are met. The Ethereum platform, released in 2015, introduced the world to a blockchain application beyond a simple transaction register—an entirely new way of managing and enforcing contracts.

6.2. Stablecoins: A Tranquil Harbour in a Stormy Sea

Investing and transacting in cryptocurrencies can be quite a roller-coaster ride due to their extreme price volatility. This volatility has led to the birth of 'Stablecoins,' digital currencies designed to minimize price fluctuations. These coins are typically pegged to a reserve of assets, such as a currency (USD, EUR, etc.) or commodities like gold. Some popular types of Stablecoins include Tether(USDT), USD Coin(USDC), and DAI.

By offering both the stability of traditional fiat currencies and the advantages of cryptocurrencies—like transparency, security, and fast transactions—Stablecoins serve as a bridge between the digital and traditional financial worlds. They are an exciting development on the digital currency frontier, bringing more people into the world of blockchain.

6.3. Privacy Coins: Raising the Anonymity Ante

While Bitcoin was initially considered anonymous, it has since been discovered that transactions using this cryptocurrency can indeed be traced and linked back to individuals. Privacy coins like Monero and

ZCash were developed to remedy this lapse, offering users added layers of privacy and anonymity.

Monero employs several privacy-enhancing technologies, such as Stealth Addresses and Ring Signatures, to ensure that neither the sender nor receiver nor the amount transacted can be discerned from the blockchain.

Conversely, ZCash provides users with the choice to either make transparent transactions, similar to Bitcoin, or shielded transactions using zk-SNARK technology to conceal the details. These privacy coins represent the digital world's deep-end, servicing users who require or desire extreme anonymity for their transactions.

6.4. Tokens: The Next Evolution in Value Exchange

Beyond digital currencies, blockchain technology also introduced the concept of tokens. These are digital assets residing on a blockchain that can represent anything from a virtual good in a game to an ownership stake in a real-world asset, like real estate. Tokens are most notably used in Initial Coin Offerings (ICOs), where projects sell them to raise funds much like companies sell shares during an Initial Public Offering (IPO).

These tokens, representing a vast array of tangible and intangible assets, offer an unprecedented level of flexibility and precision in value exchange.

6.5. The Challenges Ahead

Despite the exciting potential of these digital currencies and tokens, significant challenges remain. Regulatory uncertainty, technological complexity, cybersecurity threats, and market manipulation are amongst the hurdles hindering mass adoption.

Regulatory authorities around the world are grappling with how to manage, regulate, and tax these digital assets. This ambiguity imposes a considerable risk on investors and businesses operating in this new digital frontier.

From a technological perspective, while blockchain networks provide advanced security mechanisms, they are not entirely immune to attacks. Additionally, the complicated nature of the technology and the lack of consumer-friendly interfaces present a steep learning curve for newcomers.

Finally, market manipulation remains a significant concern. The absence of regulations and low liquidity levels make the cryptocurrency markets susceptible to pump-and-dump schemes and other manipulative tactics, eroding trust in these systems.

In conclusion, while we have already traveled far beyond Bitcoin, the journey towards greater adoption and acceptance of cryptocurrencies remains fraught with complexity. Nevertheless, these new digital frontiers, undisputedly, hold transformative potential, and the ventures pushing forward will shape our future economies and societies, crossing thresholds that were once considered fantasy. Welcome to the digital frontier—here, you steer the wheel of your financial future.

Chapter 7. The Modern Renaissance: How Crypto is Reshaping Finance

The world of finance has reached a new milestone that could evolve to be as historic as the Renaissance of the 14th century with the advent of blockchain technology and cryptocurrency. It is an innovation that is sprucing up age-old finance systems, navigating financial transactions onto a distinguished arena of transparency, security and efficiency.

7.1. The Genesis and Evolution of Crypto

In 2009, Satoshi Nakamoto introduced Bitcoin, the very first cryptocurrency, embedding within it an innovation that would later disrupt numerous industries - Blockchain. Bitcoin's core idea was to eliminate the necessity for a central authority or intermediary such as a bank or a financial institution for executing financial transactions. All transactions were now recorded on a public ledger called blockchain, which was distributed across many computers. Early sceptics were plentiful, but as time unfolded, Bitcoin began to gain recognition. It paved the way for hundreds of different cryptocurrencies to pop up, each capitalizing on different aspects of the blockchain technology.

Over a decade later, the evolution of crypto has witnessed myriad improvements and setbacks, but the wide acceptance and adoption of Bitcoin and similar assets like Ethereum, Ripple, and more have cemented cryptocurrency's place in the global financial ecosystem. As of the end of 2021, Bitcoin's market cap alone exceeds $1 trillion, underscoring the significant economic impact of the asset class.

7.2. Disruption in the Financial Industry

The disruptive potential of cryptocurrency on the financial industry is vast. The integration of blockchain technology into finance is entirely restructuring the traditional pathways, bringing in automation, transparency and decentralization.

Conventional banking has, for a long time, been plagued by delays, high transaction costs, and a lack of transparency. The traditional banking system relies on a central authority to verify transactions, which usually results in delays, especially for cross-border transfers. Cryptocurrencies, however, have been able to offer real-time transaction settlement by eliminating such intermediaries.

Large transaction fees have long been an issue with traditional finance. Blockchain technology and cryptocurrencies have made low-cost financial transactions possible, hence democratizing the financial services industry and enabling access to financial services for people worldwide, especially the unbanked population in developing countries.

7.3. Cryptocurrencies: A New Asset Class

With the rise in market capitalization of cryptocurrencies, they have forged their position as a new asset class. The digital nature of cryptocurrencies makes them immune to physical damage, loss, or theft, thus increasing their appeal. The high return potential has also garnered massive investor interest. While the degree of volatility in the cryptocurrency market deters some, others view this as an opportunity for significant capital gains. However, trading cryptocurrencies should undergo careful risk assessment due to the market's speculative nature.

7.4. The Role of DeFi and DApps

The rise of Decentralized Finance (DeFi) and Decentralized Applications (DApps), mostly built on Ethereum, has played a significant role in reshaping finance. DeFi aims to provide a fully decentralized financial system, where financial services such as loans or insurance are provided without intermediaries, based solely on smart contracts. The integration of blockchain technology into finance has given rise to platforms where financial transactions can occur without involving standard financial intermediaries, making transactions faster, cheaper and potentially more secure.

7.5. Looking Ahead: The Challenges for Crypto

Despite the promising developments, cryptocurrencies come with their own set of challenges. The promised anonymity of cryptocurrencies can be abused for activities like money laundering and illicit transactions. Furthermore, the regulatory landscape is still very much evolving and is characterized by uncertainty. The recent ban on cryptocurrencies by China and the stance of countries like India indicate a tough road ahead. Regulatory bodies have also raised concerns over the extensive energy consumption by bitcoin mining and the potential for cryptocurrencies to disrupt the existing monetary system.

The future holds numerous possibilities, and understanding these challenges will be crucial to harness the potential of blockchain technology and its implications on finance fully. Together, blockchain and cryptocurrencies hold the promise of bringing about a significant change in the world of finance, much like the renaissance brought about by the evolution of science, arts, and culture. Adoption, however, will require education, trust, and a robust regulatory framework to ensure this technology can benefit society in the best possible way. Given the pace of technological innovation and the current trajectory of crypto, the future looks set for a more decentralized, efficient and transparent financial system.

In conclusion, cryptocurrencies, DeFi and blockchain technology are indeed reshaping the financial landscape. As actors in the economic sphere - from big tech companies to startups, global banks to retail investors - continue to turn to embrace these digital assets, the impact of this modern renaissance in fintech will be both profound and enduring. Despite the challenges ahead, the pervasive effects of cryptocurrency continue to promise a brighter, more inclusive financial future for all.

Chapter 8. Major Milestones in the Blockchain Revolution: A Historical Perspective

Deciphering the origins of any new technology usually entails delving into the countless innovations and inventions that preceded its advent. The same holds for blockchain, the foundational technology underpinning cryptocurrencies, including Bitcoin, and several other applications. In the following sections, we break down pivotal moments that paved the way for this revolution, starting from the theoretical foundations to its real-world applications.

8.1. The Theoretical Foundation

The concept of blockchain technology, while visually novel, has its roots firmly established in already existing technologies. Two significant constructs form the theoretical foundation of blockchain: distributed systems and cryptography.

Distributed systems, an idea in computing where a network of independent computers function and appear as a single system, traces back to the 1960s. With the proliferation of personal computers in the 1980s, various research commenced on networked systems and distributed computing which now contributes significantly to the logic of blockchain.

Parallel to this, cryptography, the practice of secure communication in the presence of adversaries, had been advancing. With roots in ancient history, modern cryptography began to take shape in the era of digital communication. In the late 1970s, the advancements led to the creation of Public-Key Cryptography, a critical component in maintaining the security and trustless nature of blockchains.

It is these dual pillars, existing independently for decades, that eventually converged in the blockchain.

8.2. Birth of the Blockchain: The Bitcoin Whitepaper (2008)

The real birth of what we now understand as blockchain technology took place in the ominous shadow of the 2008 financial crisis. Someone, or a group, under the pseudonym 'Satoshi Nakamoto' published a whitepaper titled "Bitcoin: A Peer-to-Peer Electronic Cash System". This revolutionary paper outlined a system for a decentralized, peer-to-peer version of electronic money, allowing online payments to be sent directly without going through a financial institution.

The crux of this system, and the particular innovation that Nakamoto introduced, was blockchain. A 'chain' of 'blocks', or batches of valid transactions, that is not stored in a central location but is instead distributed across a network of computers (nodes). Each of these computers independently verifies the data integrity, making the digital trustless network possible.

Bitcoin went live in January 2009, marking the first practical implementation of blockchain technology.

8.3. Blockchain 2.0: The Birth of Ethereum and Smart Contracts (2013)

While Bitcoin pioneered blockchain and served to demonstrate its far-reaching potential, it was restricted primarily to financial transactions. A then 19-year-old Vitalik Buterin proposed a concept that would send ripples through the blockchain community and far beyond.

Recognizing the limitations of Bitcoin, Buterin conceptualized and subsequently introduced Ethereum in 2013, dreaming of something far more extensive. Ethereum envisioned the use of blockchain beyond just money transfers. In this system, blockchain could host any application's 'backend', operate 'smart contracts' (self-executing contracts with the terms of the agreement directly written into code), and create 'tokens' – unique assets or access rights managed on the blockchain.

Ethereum marked the inception of the second generation of blockchain, popularly known as Blockchain 2.0. It built on the foundations of the original blockchain, the one that powers Bitcoin, but added more complexity and functionality, enabling a myriad of potential applications.

8.4. Advancing Blockchain: From Theories to Real-World Applications (2014 – Present)

After such a breakthrough with Ethereum, there was an influx of interest and capital into this space. Numerous startups have been founded, implementing and iterating on the ideas witnessed so far.

Many variations of blockchain have sprung into existence in the form of different cryptocurrencies, each trying to improve upon the last. In 2014, Ripple challenged the status quo set by the dominant Proof Of Work concept by implementing a different system, the consensus protocol. In 2017, CryptoKitties, a game built on the Ethereum's network, demonstrated the potential of 'non-fungible tokens' (unique crypto tokens) and blockchain's applications in the gaming industry.

Major corporations such as IBM and Microsoft have poured millions into blockchain research, seeking to apply the technology to industries as broad as healthcare, logistics, and finance. Simultaneously, governments worldwide have endeavored to understand, regulate, and even embrace the potential benefits that blockchain technology offers.

Despite different purposes, these projects all share a common goal - to reach the ideal balance of security, decentralization, and scalability in blockchain.

Blockchain technology has seen an enchanting journey, from a powerful idea to a world-altering innovation in a little over a decade. While challenges remain, especially in scalability and regulatory aspects, the potential of this technology is, without doubt, colossal.

Staying attuned to the new developments and challenges in this space is invaluable. As blockchain continues to evolve and make strides toward mainstream adoption, understanding its journey and potential possibilities can help you navigate this ever-changing landscape better. Knowledge, as we say, is pivotal in this unfolding revolution, and history serves as the best teacher.

Chapter 9. Challenges to the Adoption of Cryptocurrencies and Blockchain

Blockchain technology and cryptocurrencies, undoubtedly, have the potential to transform multiple industries. With the promise of a decentralized system, better security, and enhanced transparency, they stand to revolutionize traditional financial systems. However, there are significant challenges to the broader adoption and integration of these technologies in our current financial infrastructure. The following analysis will tackle these difficulties in detail.

9.1. Technological Challenges

First and foremost, blockchain and cryptocurrencies face a number of technological hurdles.

For one, scalability remains a significant issue. Blockchain relies on a distributed ledger that requires each node in the network to store and process each transaction. This feature, while offering robust security and transparency, significantly limits the system's processing capacity. Bitcoin, one of the most well-known uses of blockchain, carries out only around seven transactions per second, which pales in comparison to Visa's capability to process 65,000 transactions per second.

One proposed solution to this issue is the implementation of "sharding," dividing the entire blockchain network into smaller pieces, each capable of processing its own transactions and smart contracts. However, it is a complex process and opens up potential avenues for security breaches.

Blockchain and cryptocurrencies also struggle with synchronization and interoperability issues. Currently, most blockchains operate independently, creating "silos" of technology that cannot interface with each other efficiently. This lack of universal standards or compatibility between different systems undermines the industry's growth prospects and ease of adoption.

Furthermore, there is a requirement for substantial computational power, particularly for proof-of-work algorithms found in many blockchain networks. This equates to significant energy consumption, leading to environmental concerns.

9.2. Regulatory Challenges

Regulation, or rather the lack of it, poses another critical challenge to mass adoption. Cryptocurrencies have long been associated with illicit activities due to their anonymous nature, underscoring the need for regulatory oversight. However, creating an appropriate regulatory framework is not straightforward, given the transnational nature of cryptocurrencies and the fast-paced evolution of the technology.

Another regulatory challenge is the definition and classification of cryptocurrencies. Different countries have different views on whether they should be treated as commodities, securities, or currencies, leading to inconsistent regulations.

9.3. Social Acceptability and Trust

Cryptocurrencies and blockchain technology rely on social acceptability for their widespread use. Despite increasing awareness, there remains a profound lack of understanding regarding the workings of this technology.

Furthermore, the volatile nature of cryptocurrencies deters potential investors. High-profile incidents, such as the bankruptcy of cryptocurrency exchange Mt. Gox because of hacking, have severely impacted the credibility and trust in this kind of digital assets. The industry needs to work hard to convince the public that it can securely manage and protect their transactions.

9.4. Economical Challenges

Cryptocurrencies confront an assortment of economic hurdles. Their volatility poses investment risks, and their value can fluctuate widely due to speculative trading and regulatory news. Consequently, this makes them less appealing as a store of value and a medium of exchange – two functions essential for any currency.

Also, the current design of tokens in many blockchains results in a lack of incentives. Miners are incentivized by the reward of new tokens or transaction fees, but as the volume of transactions increases, this model might not be sustainable in the long run.

Despite these challenges, it's important to remember that these are early days for blockchain and cryptocurrencies. Many of the hurdles highlighted here are hallmarks of a nascent technology, and innovative solutions are under development. With appropriate scaling solutions, superior energy-efficiency models, comprehensive global guidelines, and effective public education and confidence-building efforts, blockchain and cryptocurrencies can realize their revolutionary potential. Understanding these challenges is the first step toward paving the way for cryptocurrencies' adoption in mainstream finance.

Chapter 10. Future Forecast: The Prospective Developments and Trends in Crypto Finance

As we delve into the future, crypto finance, bound by the captivating blockchain technology, poses an imminent revolution. Focused on this compelling subject, this section addresses the prospective trends, developments and the vision of tomorrow that crypto finance promises.

10.1. Blockchain goes Mainstream

One of the most prominent future developments is that blockchain technology, the lynchpin behind cryptocurrencies, is poised to become mainstream. The adoption of blockchain extends beyond money transfer mechanisms, making its way towards a wide array of industries such as medical records, real estate, and even agribusiness. It brings the crucial features of transparency, decentralization, security, and speed of transactions to these fields.

10.2. Evolution of Payment Systems

With cryptocurrencies, particularly Bitcoin, gaining popularity, the next few years may witness a significant shift in how payments are made. Companies such as Tesla have already begun to accept Bitcoin as payment. This trend could create ripples in the entire finance ecosystem. It will nudge large financial institutions to adapt to and adopt this new technology, leading to the development of crypto wallets and similar facilities.

10.3. Growth of Defi (Decentralized Finance)

Decentralized finance is one of the most powerful demonstrations of blockchain technology. It seeks to remove intermediaries in financial transactions, currently occupied by financial institutions like banks and brokerage houses. As a result, it provides enormous savings in transaction costs and time. With blockchain finance, the future of Defi is unlimited – from borrowing and lending platforms to decentralized exchanges and insurance; the finance landscape can be completely remodeled.

10.4. Regulations And Crypto

Given the rapid acceleration of cryptocurrency use and the sizeable benefits, it provides, devising regulations for crypto transactions will be crucial. Regulatory bodies worldwide are working on constructing a legal framework for cryptocurrencies to safeguard users' interests and prevent misuse like money laundering. Although providing security is challenging due to the pseudonymous nature of crypto transactions, it's a task that demands urgent attention.

10.5. Cryptocurrency as an Investment Asset

Cryptocurrencies, especially Bitcoin, have been gaining popularity as a store of value. More people are treating them as 'gold replacements' in the light of economic instability. As a result, crypto finance could evolve into a significant investment industry sector in the near future.

10.6. Evolution of New Marketplaces

Building on the conceptualization of the blockchain, new marketplaces can emerge, enabling digital commerce without middlemen. An excellent example of this is the growth of NFTs (Non-Fungible Tokens), which allow for the ownership and trading of unique digital items on the blockchain.

10.7. Rising Security Measures

As the digital environment becomes more prominent, cybersecurity will become increasingly critical. Blockchain's inherent security features and the potential for further enhancements promise the development of a sturdy line of defense against hacks and digital theft.

10.8. Interoperability

Interoperability between different types of cryptocurrencies, or between blockchains themselves, could be a crucial development. This will allow seamless transfer of value between different blockchain networks, expanding the functionality and applicability of crypto finance.

In conclusion, the future of crypto finance is as exciting as it is challenging. As we foresee a surge in different uses of blockchain, we should be ready to adapt. Crypto finance promises to bring not just a radical transformation in how we understand and perceive finance, but also modifies how we trade, transact, invest, and operate in the financial world. It is truly a revolution in making. This 'challenging change' is worth embracing, for it represents not just an evolution of finance, but a fundamental shift in the mechanics of trust and value exchange.

Chapter 11. Personal Finance in the Cryptocurrency Era: A Guide to Investing in Digital Assets

The dawn of the internet age marked the beginning of a new world order characterized by digitization. In parallel, the advent of cryptocurrencies has initiated a paradigm shift within the financial ecosystems, redefining the concept of money and how it circulates within an economy. Thus began the age of Personal Finance in the cryptocurrency era.

11.1. Embracing the Digital Ledger System: Blockchain

To understand cryptocurrencies, it is essential to unpack the technology that facilitates their existence - blockchain. In its simplest form, a blockchain is a digital ledger of information. The encrypted and decentralized nature of this ledger ensures secure and tamper-resistant storage and transaction of data. This inherent security and transparency make blockchain the backbone of cryptocurrencies. A cryptocurrency is essentially a digital or virtual form of currency that uses encryption for security.

11.2. The Allure of Cryptocurrency: Drawing Investors

In a conventional economy, the state controls the supply and value of currency. In contrast, cryptocurrencies are decentralized, with no central authority controlling its supply or value. This decentralization is a double-edged sword. On one hand, it provides protection from inflation and independence from state monetary policies, and on the other hand, it introduces market risks such as volatile price fluctuations. Yet, the potential for high returns has allured many investors towards this relatively new investment vehicle.

Cryptocurrencies are fundamentally different from traditional forms of investment. Unlike stocks and bonds, they do not provide any ownership interest or rights to future cash flows. Their value is driven purely by demand and supply. When investing in cryptocurrencies, you're essentially betting that the demand for the selected cryptocurrency will increase in the future.

11.3. Understanding Investment Strategies for Cryptocurrencies

When investing in cryptocurrencies, several strategies can be employed. Let's delve into the two most popular ones:

1. **Long-Term Investing or 'Hodling'** The term 'Hodling' comes from a misspelled word in a forum message by an early Bitcoin investor. It has since become a widely accepted term in the cryptocurrency culture, referring to holding a cryptocurrency over a long period, regardless of market fluctuations.

2. **Day Trading** Day-trading involves making many trades within a single trading day, with the objective to benefit from short-term price fluctuations. Day-trading demands constant attention and swift decision-making.

11.4. Navigating Cryptocurrency Exchanges

Cryptocurrencies are traded on digital platforms called cryptocurrency exchanges. They function as marketplaces where individuals can buy, sell, or trade their cryptocurrencies. The sheer number of exchanges, each with its distinct characteristics and features, can be daunting for beginner investors. Examples of popular exchanges include Binance, Coinbase, and Kraken.

11.5. Wallets: Your Personal Cryptocurrency Bank

To store your cryptocurrencies, you'll need a digital wallet. These wallets can be online (web-based or on your mobile), offline (desktop application or hardware device), or even paper-based. Each has its advantages and risks, and your choice will depend on your security comfort level and ease-of-use preference.

11.6. Understanding and Mitigating Risk

Investing in cryptocurrencies carries inherent risks. The volatility of the market can lead to significant monetary losses in a short span. The decentralization, while providing benefits, also means that legal recourse in case of fraud or loss can be complicated and usually unsuccessful. Therefore, risk mitigation strategies must be in place before investing. These include diversification, setting stop losses, and only investing what you're willing to lose.

11.7. Taxation and Legal Aspects of Cryptocurrency Investments

Recognizing cryptocurrencies for their potential, many countries have started legislating the use and trade of cryptocurrencies, including their taxation. Some countries have embraced them with open arms while others have banned them outright. Thus, it's imperative to understand the specific laws applied to cryptocurrencies in your jurisdiction before you start investing.

11.8. Future Outlook: Will Cryptocurrencies Lead the Finance Game?

The future of cryptocurrencies is highly speculative. Optimists believe that with increasing acceptance and legislation, cryptocurrencies will become mainstream, replacing traditional currency and revolutionizing the finance world. Pessimists, however, think cryptocurrencies are a bubble, destined to burst. The middle ground, the pragmatists, believe that while cryptocurrencies may not entirely replace traditional currency, they will co-exist and influence significant aspects of finance.

In conclusion, investing in cryptocurrencies is an exciting prospect filled with opportunities and challenges. Thorough knowledge, careful planning, and risk mitigation strategies can provide a significant edge in navigating this relatively new investment landscape. The potential rewards are enormous, but so are the risks. As with any investment, it's recommended to invest wisely, and the information provided in this chapter will empower you to make informed decisions in your cryptocurrency journey.

www.ingramcontent.com/pod-product-compliance
Lightning Source LLC
Chambersburg PA
CBHW071042260726
48661CB00007B/3107